RONALDO & MESSI

202 FASCINATING FACTS, INTRIGUING TRIVIA,
AND CAPTIVATING STORIES FOR FANS

FAME FOCUS

CONTENTS

Introduction   v

1. Ronaldo Facts   1
2. Trivia Questions   23
3. Trivia Answers   37
4. Ronaldo Quiz Scorecard   41
5. Messi Facts   43
6. Trivia Questions   69
7. Trivia Answers   83
8. Messi's Quiz Scorecard   87
9. Messi VS. Ronaldo   89
10. Who's the best?   91

INTRODUCTION

Welcome to *Ronaldo & Messi*, a book where the world of football's two most iconic stars, Cristiano Ronaldo and Lionel Messi, comes alive in a vivid and engaging compilation. This is not just a book; it's a celebration of two unparalleled journeys that have redefined the boundaries of what's possible in the world of football.

In these pages, we delve into the lives of Ronaldo and Messi, unearthing stories that go beyond the football pitch. From Ronaldo's journey from the rugged streets of Madeira to the bright lights of Manchester and Madrid to Messi's ascent from the quiet neighborhoods of Rosario to the grandeur of Barcelona and Paris, their stories are about more than just goals and glory. They are tales of perseverance, dedication, and the relentless pursuit of greatness.

As you navigate through the 202 entries, you will discover a blend of facts that are as astonishing as they are true, trivia that challenges and delights, and stories that paint a picture of two athletes who have not just scored goals, but also won hearts worldwide. Each fact, trivia, and story is carefully chosen to offer a holistic view of Ronaldo and Messi, not just as footballers, but as global icons who have influenced the sport and its fans in innumerable ways.

Whether you are a die-hard fan of Ronaldo's power and precision or Messi's agility and creativity, or simply a lover of the beautiful game, this book is for you. It's an invitation to look beyond the trophies and accolades, to understand what makes these players the legends they are. It's a journey through the highs and lows, the records and achievements, the passion and dedication of two of the greatest footballers the world has ever seen.

Prepare to be surprised, informed, and inspired as you turn each page. *Ronaldo & Messi* is more than a book - it's a tribute to the spirit of football, embodied by Ronaldo and Messi.

1

RONALDO FACTS

1 Cristiano Ronaldo's full name is Cristiano Ronaldo dos Santos Aveiro. He was born on February 5, 1985, on the small island of Madeira, Portugal.

2 He was born into a humble family and is the youngest of four children of Maria Dolores dos Santos Aveiro and José Dinis Aveiro.

3 Cristiano Ronaldo's father, José Dinis Aveiro, worked as a municipal gardener and was also a part-time kit man for Andorinha, the local football club where Ronaldo first played. José struggled with alcoholism and passed away in 2005 due to liver failure.

4 His mother, Maria Dolores dos Santos Aveiro, worked as a cook to help support the family. She played a crucial role in Ronaldo's life, encouraging his football talents and often taking him to training sessions and matches in his early years.

5 Ronaldo's older brother, Hugo, has worked on projects related to Ronaldo's CR7 brand and museum.

6 Cristiano has two older sisters, Elma and Liliana Cátia. Elma is involved in the family business, particularly managing Ronaldo's CR7 fashion brand, while Liliana Cátia, also known as Katia Aveiro, is a singer in Portugal and has released several albums.

7 Cristiano Ronaldo was named after Ronald Reagan, a favorite actor of his father's, as his parents appreciated the name's strength and resonance long before Reagan became the President of the United States.

8 As a child, Ronaldo earned the nicknames 'Cry Baby' and 'Little Bee' from his family and friends; 'Cry Baby' due to his tendency to cry when his passes didn't lead to goals, and 'Little Bee' for his notable speed, a trait that continued to define his playing style throughout his career.

9 At the age of eight, Cristiano Ronaldo started playing football, joining the amateur team Andorinha in Madeira, Portugal.

10 At the age of 14, Cristiano Ronaldo was expelled from school after he threw a chair at his teacher, citing disrespect as the reason for his actions. Although this incident had negative consequences, it marked a

significant turning point in his life. Encouraged by his mother, he channeled all his attention into soccer, a decision that ultimately propelled him to become an international sensation in football.

11 At the young age of 15, Ronaldo underwent critical heart surgery to address his diagnosed condition of Tachycardia, a rapid heartbeat exceeding 100 beats per minute that posed risks of stroke or heart failure. As his mother recounted to the Daily Mail in 2009, doctors utilized a laser technique to cauterize the source of the issue, allowing for a swift surgery that saw Ronaldo leave the hospital by the afternoon of the same day.

12 His professional football career began in 2002 when he debuted for Sporting CP in Portugal. He was just 17 years old.

13 In 2003, Ronaldo's exceptional talent caught the attention of Manchester United, leading to his signing for a then-record fee of £12.24 million for a teenager, marking his entry into the English Premier League.

14 At Manchester, he became renowned for his signature move, the 'Ronaldo Chop,' a skillful step-over technique frequently used to outmaneuver defenders during matches.

15 During his time at Manchester United, Ronaldo won three consecutive Premier League titles in the 2006-07, 2007-08, and 2008-09 seasons.

16 In the 2007-08 season, Ronaldo played a pivotal role in helping Manchester United secure the UEFA Champions League title.

17 Ronaldo clinched his first FIFA Club World Cup in December 2008 with Manchester United.

18 He was awarded his first Ballon d'Or in 2008, recognizing him as the best player in the world.

19 In 2009, Cristiano Ronaldo made a historic transfer to Real Madrid for a then-world record fee of £80 million, marking the most expensive football transfer at that time.

20 Ronaldo spent nine seasons with Real Madrid, during which he became the club's all-time leading scorer.

21 During Ronaldo's time at Real Madrid, he won four Champions League titles.

22 He was ranked third in the 'World Player of the Decade 2000s,' behind Lionel Messi and Ronaldinho.

23 Cristiano Ronaldo won his first trophy with Real Madrid during the 2010-11 season, securing the Copa del Rey. This victory marked an important milestone in his career with the club, as it was his first piece of silverware in the famous white jersey of Real Madrid.

24 In the following season, 2011-12, Ronaldo secured his first La Liga title with Real Madrid.

25 The 2012-13 season saw Ronaldo winning the Supercopa de España with Real Madrid.

26 He won his second Ballon d'Or in the 2013-14 season.

27 In the same season, Ronaldo also won another Copa del Rey and his second Champions League, setting a record with 17 goals in the tournament.

28 Ronaldo received his third Ballon d'Or in 2014, along with his second FIFA Club World Cup in December of the same year.

29 In 2016, he won his third Champions League with Real Madrid. He scored the winning penalty in the final against Atlético Madrid.

30 The following season, Ronaldo earned his fourth Ballon d'Or, won another La Liga title after five years, secured another Champions League trophy, and achieved his second Club World Cup.

31 His last season with Real Madrid, 2017-18, was marked by his fifth Ballon d'Or in 2017 and his fifth Champions League title, including scoring twice in the final against Juventus.

32 Ronaldo set a record as the first player to win the UEFA Champions League five times.

33 He transferred to Juventus in July 2018, leaving Real Madrid as its all-time top goal scorer and the only player in La Liga history to score 30 or more goals in six consecutive seasons.

34 Ronaldo began his international career with Portugal at age 18 and scored his first goal at UEFA Euro 2004, helping Portugal reach the final.

35 He played in his first World Cup in 2006, contributing to Portugal's fourth-place finish.

36 Ronaldo became the full captain of Portugal in 2008 and has since participated in four European Championships (2008, 2012, 2016, 2020) and three FIFA World Cups (2014, 2018, 2022).

37 During his youth, Cristiano Ronaldo greatly admired Brazilian football legends Ronaldinho and Ronaldo Nazário. He often regarded them as his idols and publicly stated they left "a beautiful history in football."

38 Cristiano Ronaldo, while naturally right-footed and exceptionally versatile on the field, capable of playing on both wings and as a striker, says he prefers the forward position, where he can best leverage his prolific goal-scoring skills.

39 Ronaldo, celebrated for his lightning speed, has been clocked reaching impressive velocities on the pitch, with recorded speeds of up to 20.9 miles per hour (33.6 kilometers per hour), distinguishing him as one of the fastest football players in the world.

40 Cristiano stands over 6 feet tall and combines his height with an exceptional vertical leap, reportedly measuring up to 30.7 inches (78 cm), amplifying his

already impressive heading ability. This combination makes him a formidable aerial threat in football, capable of out-jumping defenders and goalkeepers alike.

41 Ronaldo is celebrated for mastering the 'knuckleball' free kick technique, where he strikes the ball to minimize spin, causing it to move erratically in the air. This method, difficult for goalkeepers to predict and defend, has led to some spectacular goals. Ronaldo's free kicks often clocked at  speeds exceeding 80 miles per hour (130 kilometers per hour).

42 Ronaldo has scored 140 penalty kicks in his professional club and international career. This figure includes penalties scored for Sporting CP, Manchester United, Real Madrid, Juventus, and the Portugal national team.

43 He has scored 60 hat-tricks in his professional career for club and country.

44 Cristiano Ronaldo's signature "Siu" celebration, a dynamic jump accompanied by a confident shout of "Siu" – meaning "Yes" in Spanish – first debuted in 2013 during a match with Real Madrid against Chelsea in the International Champions Cup,

symbolizing his exuberant joy and triumph upon scoring.

45 Cristiano Ronaldo has achieved a remarkable milestone of 807 career goals, surpassing Josef Bican's previous record of 805 goals set between 1931 and 1955, thus establishing Ronaldo as the highest-ever goalscorer in the history of men's soccer.

46 Cristiano Ronaldo has achieved the remarkable feat of scoring 145 goals with his head across his tenures at five clubs and the Portugal national team.

47 Ronaldo's astonishing athletic prowess was displayed when he achieved his highest recorded jump of 9 feet 7 inches (2.93m) against Manchester United in the 2012-13 UEFA Champions League while playing for Real Madrid. Given Ronaldo's height of 6 feet 2 inches (1.87m), this jump translates to a remarkable vertical leap of approximately 41.7 inches (1.06m).

48 In a Champions League quarter-final match against Juventus, Cristiano Ronaldo scored a stunning bicycle kick goal, widely celebrated as one of the most incredible goals in the tournament's history.

49 In 2009, Real Madrid took steps to protect their investment in Ronaldo by insuring his legs for a reported sum of around €100 million.

50 Ronaldo's training regimen, distinguished by its intensity and thoroughness, includes five weekly sessions, each lasting 3 to 4 hours, and encompasses

cardio exercises, weight training, football drills, and high-intensity interval training (HIIT) to enhance his speed, strength, agility, and explosive power.

51 Complementing his rigorous workout routine, Ronaldo incorporates core strength exercises, swimming, and Pilates into his regime for balance, recovery, and flexibility. He often exceeds his team's training schedule with additional individual sessions to ensure continuous improvement and peak fitness.

52 Cristiano's diet, crucial to his training, is meticulously planned with multiple small meals a day, rich in protein, carbohydrates, and healthy fats. He focuses on lean meats, whole grains, fresh fruits, and vegetables while avoiding sugary foods and alcohol to ensure optimal recovery and peak performance.

53 Cristiano Ronaldo incorporates mental exercises, such as meditation and visualization techniques, into his training regimen, enhancing his focus and

competitive edge. These practices help him mentally prepare for matches, stay calm under pressure, and visualize successful outcomes, contributing significantly to his on-field performance and decision-making.

54 Ronaldo is known for his generous philanthropic efforts, notably donating €1.5 million to fund a pediatric hospital in Madeira, his hometown, in 2017.

55 In 2015, Ronaldo was named the world's most charitable sportsperson after donating a substantial amount of money to various causes, including €5 million to the relief efforts following the earthquake in Nepal.

56 He frequently contributes to children's charities, like Save the Children, and has funded schools in war zones, demonstrating his commitment to improving the lives of underprivileged children.

57 Ronaldo has also been involved in campaigns for blood donation and bone marrow donation, using his global influence to raise awareness about these important causes.

58 Cristiano has consciously chosen not to have any tattoos on his body, a decision influenced by his commitment to regularly donating blood. By avoiding tattoos, he ensures that he doesn't have to contend with the mandatory waiting periods that can follow tattooing, thus enabling him to donate blood more frequently and continue supporting this vital cause.

59 In response to the COVID-19 pandemic, Ronaldo and his agent, Jorge Mendes, donated significant funds to hospitals in Portugal for critical care beds and medical equipment.

60 Ronaldo was raised in a devout Catholic family, and his faith has been an important aspect of his life. While he is not publicly outspoken about his religious beliefs, he has been known to make gestures on the field that suggest a deep personal faith. For instance, he often makes the cross sign before games, a common practice among Catholic athletes.

61 Cristiano Ronaldo's foray into the world of fragrances is marked by the launch of his signature line, 'CR7 Fragrances.' This collection includes a range of scents designed to reflect Ronaldo's style and charisma. The flagship product, 'CR7 Eau de Toilette,' was first introduced in 2017. It is described as a modern, sporty fragrance with notes of lavender, apple, and cinnamon, making it suitable for everyday wear.

62 In 2003, before rising to global fame, Cristiano Ronaldo appeared in a television commercial for 'Super Bock,' a well-known Portuguese clothing brand. At the time, Ronaldo was just beginning to make his mark in the world of football, and this commercial represented one of his earliest ventures into the realm of brand endorsements.

63 In 2017, Ronaldo was accused by Spanish authorities of tax evasion, involving €14.7 million in image rights income channeled through offshore companies. He settled the case in 2019, accepting a two-year suspended jail sentence and agreeing to pay €18.8 million in fines, thereby avoiding jail time.

64 Cristiano's intensely competitive nature on the field has led to several red cards and criticism for his behavior, including contentious reactions to referee decisions and confrontations with opponents. His aggressive playing style and occasional dramatics in drawing fouls have sparked debates about sportsmanship in football.

65 As a global ambassador for Clear Shampoo and Herbalife, Ronaldo uses his widespread popularity to promote hair care and health and wellness products, showcasing his diverse brand appeal.

66 Ronaldo has aligned with TAG Heuer, representing their high-end Swiss watches, and partnered with DAZN, a sports streaming service in the luxury and digital media sectors, to promote their extensive sports coverage.

67 Expanding his business ventures, Ronaldo has collaborated with American Tourister in the travel industry, co-owns CR7 Hotels in partnership with the Pestana Hotel Group, and endorses MTG's healthcare and fitness products, reflecting his entrepreneurial spirit and commitment to a lifestyle of health and luxury.

68 Cristiano Ronaldo's hair, known for its frequent and varied styles ranging from sleek combed-back looks to edgy spiked designs, has become almost as iconic as his football skills. His zigzag pattern during the 2014 World Cup stood out, trending among fans and media. Often a form of personal expression, his hairstyles are widely imitated globally, enhancing his influence beyond football.

69 Cristiano's avid interest in luxury vehicles is reflected in his impressive collection of exclusive sports cars, including rare models like the Bugatti Veyron, Lamborghini Aventador, Ferrari F12, and the standout $3 million Bugatti Chiron, known for its exceptional speed and engineering, epitomizing his taste for style and high performance.

70 Since 2016, Cristiano Ronaldo has been under a lifetime endorsement deal with Nike, valued at $1 billion. He is the third athlete after LeBron James and Michael Jordan to secure such a significant agreement. Forbes reported that in 2016, Ronaldo's social media presence generated an astounding $474 million in value for Nike through 329 posts, underlining his immense marketing influence.

71 Ronaldo owns a private jet, which he uses to travel efficiently for professional football matches and personal commitments. This jet allows him the flexibility and convenience to manage his busy schedule, attend various events worldwide, and balance his high-profile career and personal life.

72 Inaugurated in 2013, the CR7 Museum in Cristiano Ronaldo's birthplace of Funchal, Madeira, is a tribute to the soccer star's illustrious career and life. The museum showcases a comprehensive collection, including photographs from Ronaldo's childhood and his accumulated trophies, medals, and even soccer balls from notable matches.

73 Ronaldo has scored 60 free-kick goals in his professional career. His 'knuckleball' free-kick technique makes the ball move unpredictably in flight, challenging goalkeepers.

74 Cristiano Ronaldo's relationship with Georgina Rodriguez began in 2016 when they first met at a Gucci store in Madrid. Georgina worked as a shop assistant at 22 while Ronaldo was 31.

75 Cristiano's family includes his first child, Cristiano Jr., born in June 2010, over whom Ronaldo has full custody, with the mother's identity kept private. In June 2017, he expanded his family by welcoming twins Eva and Mateo, who were born via surrogacy.

76 Later, in 2017, Ronaldo's family grew once more when his partner, Georgina Rodriguez, gave birth to their daughter Alana Martina in November, marking Ronaldo's fourth child.

77 Cristiano Ronaldo strongly emphasizes family values, consistently highlighting their importance in his life. He frequently dedicates quality time to his children and partner, engaging in simple yet meaningful activities such as playing games and relaxing together at home.

78 In 2020, he made history by becoming the first active team-sport athlete to surpass $1 billion in career earnings, as reported by Forbes.

79 Cristiano Ronaldo has a penchant for traveling to various stunning destinations worldwide. His favorite vacation spots have included Ibiza, Miami, Dubai, Paris, Madeira (his hometown), Greece, Las Vegas, and the Maldives. These destinations offer a glimpse into his diverse travel interests, from vibrant nightlife to tropical paradises, reflecting his love for exploration and relaxation.

80 Cristiano Ronaldo actively participates in prominent fashion events, including fashion weeks in cities like Paris and Milan and gatherings hosted by renowned brands like Dolce & Gabbana and Versace.

81 He has actively participated in professional poker tournaments and promotional poker events. However, no widely reported significant poker winnings are associated with his involvement. His interest in poker is more about enjoyment and brand promotion rather than substantial monetary gains.

82 Cristiano frequently attends concerts by artists such as Rihanna and Jennifer Lopez, sharing his music preferences on social media. His global prominence has also resulted in collaborations with musicians, exemplified by his appearances in music

videos and promotional campaigns, like those for Ricky Martin.

83 Ronaldo has shared the pitch with several notable players, including Wayne Rooney, Ryan Giggs, and Paul Scholes, during his time at Manchester United, forming a formidable partnership that contributed to multiple Premier League titles and Champions League success.

84 At Real Madrid, Ronaldo played alongside Sergio Ramos, Luka Modrić, and Karim Benzema, achieving great success. His international rivalry with Lionel Messi has also produced iconic clashes when representing Portugal and Argentina.

85 Throughout his career, Ronaldo has faced a series of significant injuries and setbacks, including an ankle injury during the 2008 UEFA European Championship, a knee injury while at Real Madrid in 2014, a thigh injury in 2019 while playing for Juventus, and a period of COVID-19 isolation in 2020. In each instance, Ronaldo showcased his resilience and determination, swiftly recovering and returning to the field to maintain his high level of performance.

86 He boasts the most-viewed Wikipedia page for a male athlete, with a staggering 112 million views. He is also the fourth most followed person on Twitter, with 110 million followers.

87 Ronaldo's mentorship extends to nurturing young and lesser-known talents at Manchester United and

Real Madrid. His guidance and belief in players like Danny Welbeck, Federico Macheda, Lucas Vázquez, and Marco Asensio have been instrumental in their development, boosting their confidence and helping them thrive in top-level football.

88 Cristiano Ronaldo's close friends among famous personalities include former Manchester United teammates Patrice Evra and Rio Ferdinand, UFC fighter Conor McGregor, and Hollywood actor Dwayne 'The Rock' Johnson.

89 Known for his accessibility, Ronaldo often grants fans requests for selfies and autographs, making time for personal interactions at training sessions, airports, and public events. He engages actively with his global fan base on social media, personally responding to comments and messages, strengthening his connection with supporters worldwide.

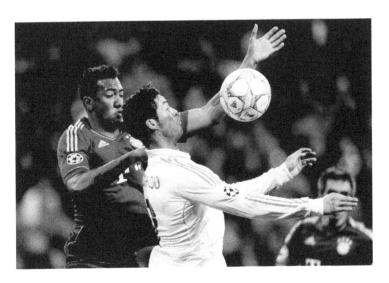

90 Cristiano Ronaldo is proficient in several languages beyond Portuguese, including English, Spanish, and Italian. These language skills have facilitated his international football career and allowed him to connect with fans and teammates from different backgrounds and cultures.

91 Ronaldo has made a substantial community impact in his hometown of Madeira, Portugal, through donations to the local hospital, the creation of the CR7 Museum, youth development programs, and charitable work via the Cristiano Ronaldo Foundation. His efforts have positively influenced the region's healthcare, tourism, education, and youth empowerment.

92 Cristiano is an animal lover who owns several dog breeds, including bulldogs and labrador retrievers, frequently sharing his affection for his canine companions on social media.

93 Ronaldo's early mentors were instrumental in his football journey. Sporting CP provided essential guidance during his formative years, while at Manchester United, legendary manager Sir Alex Ferguson coached and mentored him. Additionally, Carlos Queiroz, the assistant manager at Manchester United, played a vital role in Ronaldo's development as a top-level footballer through coaching and guidance.

94 In FIFA 18, Ronaldo held the top spot as the highest-rated player with an impressive overall rating

of 99%, placing him 1% ahead of runners-up Lionel Messi and Pelé, who both had ratings of 98%.

95 Cristiano's legendary association with the number 7 jersey has left an indelible mark on his career. At Manchester United, he inherited this iconic number, previously worn by club legends like George Best, Eric Cantona, and David Beckham.

96 Famous for his meticulous nature, Ronaldo adheres to a set of superstitious habits. These rituals range from stepping onto the pitch with his right foot to carefully styling his hair before every match, all of which have become integral components of his pre-game routine.

97 Upon his arrival at Manchester United in 2003, Cristiano Ronaldo had a limited grasp of English. He required a translator to communicate with his manager, Sir Alex Ferguson. Ronaldo humorously remarked that even to this day, he finds it challenging to understand Ferguson's Scottish accent. In the early days, he relied on a Brazilian translator primarily for interactions with his manager.

98 Cristiano became the fourth footballer to be represented as a waxwork at Madame Tussauds in London. He joined the ranks of other football legends like Steven Gerrard, Pelé, and David Beckham, who had also been honored with wax figures at the famous museum. These wax statues are created to commemorate the achievements and popularity of notable individuals in various fields, including sports.

99 Ronaldo holds the record as the most-followed individual, male figure, sports personality, and European personality on Instagram, boasting an impressive following of over 612 million users.

100 Throughout his distinguished career, Cristiano Ronaldo has continually evolved his playing style, starting as a winger at Manchester United, where he focused on delivering crosses, then transitioning to a more central striker role at Real Madrid with an emphasis on goal-scoring, and finally at Juventus, where he combined his role as a prolific target man with a return to more active dribbling and crossing, occasionally revisiting his roots as a winger to engage defenders directly.

101 Cristiano Ronaldo has stated his ambition to continue playing football at the highest level well into his late 30s, demonstrating his commitment to maintaining peak physical condition and performance.

2

TRIVIA QUESTIONS

1) What is Cristiano Ronaldo's full name?

a) Cristiano Ronaldo Aveiro

b) Cristiano Ronaldo dos Santos Aveiro

c) Cristiano Ronaldo Silva

d) Cristiano Ronaldo Fernandez

2) Who was Ronaldo's role model and the inspiration behind his name?

a) Lionel Messi

b) Cristiano Ronaldo Sr.

c) Ronaldinho

d) Ronald Reagan

3) What was Cristiano Ronaldo's nickname as a child due to his speed?

a) Little Bee

b) Speedy Gonzales

c) Flash

d) Bolt

4) At what age did Cristiano Ronaldo start playing football for Andorinha?

a) 8

b) 10

c) 12

d) 14

5) What medical condition did Cristiano Ronaldo undergo heart surgery for at the age of 15?

a) Broken arm

b) Tachycardia

c) Asthma

d) Migraine

6) In which year did Cristiano Ronaldo make his professional debut for Sporting CP?

a) 2000

b) 2002

c) 2004

d) 2006

7) Which club signed Cristiano Ronaldo for a then-record fee of £12.24 million when he was 18 years old?

a) FC Barcelona

b) Manchester United

c) Real Madrid

d) Sporting CP

8) What was Cristiano Ronaldo's signature move, known for outmaneuvering defenders?

a) Bicycle Kick

b) Rainbow Flick

c) Ronaldo Chop

d) Scorpion Kick

9) During his time at Manchester United, in which season did Cristiano Ronaldo help the club secure the UEFA Champions League title?

a) 2005-06

b) 2006-07

c) 2007-08

d) 2008-09

10) What was the world-record transfer fee when Cristiano Ronaldo transferred from Manchester United to Real Madrid in 2009?

a) £40 million

b) £60 million

c) £80 million

d) £100 million

11) In which season did Cristiano Ronaldo win his second Ballon d'Or award?

a) 2011-12

b) 2012-13

c) 2013-14

d) 2014-15

12) How many UEFA Champions League titles did Ronaldo win during his time with Real Madrid?

a) 2

b) 3

c) 4

d) 5

13) When did Cristiano Ronaldo become the full captain of the Portugal national team?

a) 2004

b) 2006

c) 2008

d) 2010

14) Who were Cristiano Ronaldo's idols and football legends during his youth?

a) Diego Maradona and Pelé

b) Lionel Messi and Neymar

c) Ronaldinho and Ronaldo Nazário

d) Zinedine Zidane and David Beckham

15) What is Cristiano Ronaldo's preferred position on the field?

a) Midfielder

b) Defender

c) Forward

d) Goalkeeper

16) What is the fastest recorded speed that Cristiano Ronaldo reached on the pitch?

a) 18.5 miles per hour

b) 20.9 miles per hour

c) 22.5 miles per hour

d) 24.3 miles per hour

17) How many career goals has Cristiano Ronaldo scored with his head?

a) 50

b) 75

c) 100

d) 145

18) What is the significance of Cristiano Ronaldo's "Siu" celebration?

a) It means "No" in Spanish.

b) It symbolizes victory and joy.

c) It's a tribute to his favorite football club.

d) It's a message to his teammates.

19) What record did Cristiano Ronaldo set in the UEFA Champions League?

a) Most assists in a single season

b) Most goals in a single season

c) Most consecutive hat-tricks

d) Most penalties scored

20) How many hat-tricks has Cristiano Ronaldo scored in his professional career for club and country?

a) 30

b) 45

c) 60

d) 75

21) How many weekly training sessions does Cristiano Ronaldo typically undergo?

a) 2 to 3

b) 3 to 4

c) 5 to 6

d) 7

22) What type of training is NOT part of Cristiano Ronaldo's workout regimen?

a) Weight training

b) Swimming

c) Yoga

d) High-intensity interval training (HIIT)

23) What does Ronaldo primarily focus on in his diet to support his training?

a) Sugary foods and alcohol

b) Lean meats and whole grains

c) Processed snacks and fast food

d) Carbonated beverages and fried foods

24) Besides physical exercises, what other techniques does Cristiano Ronaldo incorporate into his training regimen?

a) Cooking lessons

b) Meditation and visualization

c) Dancing

d) Singing

25) In 2017, Cristiano Ronaldo donated €1.5 million to fund what in his hometown of Madeira?

a) A soccer stadium

b) A pediatric hospital

c) A school for the arts

d) A public library

26) What major natural disaster prompted Cristiano Ronaldo to donate €5 million to relief efforts in 2015?

a) Hurricane

b) Earthquake in Nepal

c) Tsunami

d) Tornado

27) Which cause has Cristiano Ronaldo NOT been involved in campaigning for?

a) Blood donation

b) Bone marrow donation

c) Cancer research

d) Child welfare

28) Why has Cristiano Ronaldo chosen not to have tattoos on his body?

a) He is afraid of needles.

b) He doesn't like the look of tattoos.

c) To avoid mandatory waiting periods for blood donation

d) To stand out from other football players

29) What significant donation did Cristiano Ronaldo and his agent Jorge Mendes make in response to the COVID-19 pandemic?

a) Donated ventilators to hospitals

b) Funded a new vaccine research center

c) Supported critical care beds and medical equipment in Portugal

d) Provided free masks to the public

30) What gesture does Cristiano Ronaldo often make before games, reflecting his faith?

a) Saluting the crowd

b) Kissing the ball

c) Making the cross sign

d) Doing a cartwheel

31) How many children does Cristiano Ronaldo have?

a) 2

b) 3

c) 4

d) 5

32) When were Cristiano Ronaldo's twins, Eva and Mateo, born?

a) June 2010

b) June 2017

c) November 2017

d) July 2018

33) Who is Cristiano Ronaldo's partner and the mother of his daughter Alana Martina?

a) Georgina Rodriguez

b) Irina Shayk

c) Alessandra Ambrosio

d) Shakira

34) What significant financial milestone did Cristiano Ronaldo achieve in 2020?

a) $100 million in career earnings

b) $500 million in career earnings

c) $1 billion in career earnings

d) $10 billion in career earnings

35) Which of the following destinations is NOT mentioned as one of Cristiano Ronaldo's favorite vacation spots?

a) Ibiza

b) Paris

c) Moscow

d) Maldives

36) In addition to football, Cristiano Ronaldo actively participates in which other area of interest?

a) Professional poker

b) Cooking

c) Chess

d) Painting

37) Which artists have Cristiano Ronaldo publicly mentioned attending concerts of?

a) Elvis Presley and Frank Sinatra

b) Rihanna and Jennifer Lopez

c) The Beatles and Queen

d) Beyoncé and Justin Bieber

38) During his time at Manchester United, which players formed a notable partnership with Cristiano Ronaldo?

a) Lionel Messi and Neymar

b) Wayne Rooney and Ryan Giggs

c) Sergio Ramos and Luka Modrić

d) Zinedine Zidane and David Beckham

39) How has Cristiano Ronaldo demonstrated his resilience and determination in his career?

a) By becoming a professional poker champion

b) By consistently avoiding injuries

c) By swiftly recovering from injuries and setbacks

d) By switching to a career in music

40) Cristiano Ronaldo's signature celebration, where he jumps and shouts "Siu," first debuted in 2013 during a match with which club?

a) Manchester United

b) Real Madrid

c) Sporting CP

d) Juventus

3

TRIVIA ANSWERS

1. b) Cristiano Ronaldo dos Santos Aveiro

2. d) Ronald Reagan

3. a) Little Bee

4. a) 8

5. b) Tachycardia

6. b) 2002

7. b) Manchester United

8. c) Ronaldo Chop

9. c) 2007-08

10. c) £80 million

11. c) 2013-14

12. d) 5

13. c) 2008

14. c) Ronaldinho and Ronaldo Nazário

15. c) Forward

16. b) 20.9 miles per hour

17. d) 145

18. b) It symbolizes victory and joy.

19. b) Most goals in a single season

20. c) 60

21. b) 3 to 4

22. c) Yoga

23. b) Lean meats and whole grains

24. b) Meditation and visualization

25. b) A pediatric hospital

26. b) Earthquake in Nepal

27. c) Cancer research

28. c) To avoid mandatory waiting periods for blood donation

29. c) Supported critical care beds and medical equipment in Portugal

30. c) Making the cross sign

31. c) 4

32. b) June 2017

33. a) Georgina Rodriguez

34. c) $1 billion in career earnings

35. c) Moscow

36. a) Professional poker

37. b) Rihanna and Jennifer Lopez

38. b) Wayne Rooney and Ryan Giggs

39. c) By swiftly recovering from injuries and setbacks

40. b) Real Madrid

4

RONALDO QUIZ SCORECARD

Score __/40

16-20: Room for Improvement

You're on the right track, but there's more to discover about Ronaldo. Keep learning, and you'll get better!

21-25: Not Bad!

You've got a fair understanding of Cristiano Ronaldo. Keep exploring, and you'll improve even more!

26-30: Good Going!

You know quite a bit about Ronaldo. Keep learning and you'll become an expert in no time!

31-35: Great Job!

You've got a fantastic knowledge of Cristiano Ronaldo. Keep up the good work!

36-40: You're a Pro!

Wow, you really know Cristiano Ronaldo inside out. You're a true Ronaldo expert!

5

MESSI FACTS

1 Messi's full name is Lionel Andrés Messi Cuccitini. He was born on June 24, 1987, in Rosario, Argentina. He grew up in a football-loving family in a city that's also the birthplace of other famous Argentinian footballers like Ángel Di María.

2 Lionel's father, Jorge Messi, was deeply involved in his son's football journey. As a local steel factory manager, he balanced work with coaching Lionel and his brothers in their early football endeavors.

3 Celia Cuccittini, Lionel's mother, played a pivotal nurturing role. While working part-time as a cleaner, she provided strong emotional support and encouragement, vital in Lionel's development as a person and an athlete.

4 Lionel Messi, the third of four children, has a significant age gap with his siblings. Born in 1979, Rodrigo is eight years his senior and manages Lionel's professional schedule. Matías, born in 1982, five years

older, oversees his charitable foundation. María Sol, his younger sister, born in 1993, six years his junior, maintains a private life but shares a close bond with Lionel.

5 Lionel Messi started playing soccer at a young age, around 4 years old. He joined a local club, Grandoli, where his father coached him.

6 At age 8, Lionel Messi joined Newell's Old Boys, a prominent football club in his hometown, Rosario, where his exceptional talent quickly set him apart as a prodigious young player in the football world.

7 Lionel Messi was diagnosed with idiopathic short stature, a type of growth hormone deficiency, around the age of 10. This condition hindered his growth and physical development, making him noticeably smaller and shorter than his peers. His treatment involved regular injections of growth hormones to help normalize his growth.

8 Facing financial challenges, Lionel Messi's family approached River Plate, a prominent Argentinian football club, for assistance with his costly growth hormone treatments. Despite River Plate's interest in Messi's talent, they could not fund his medical needs either.

9 In 2000, at the age of 13, Lionel Messi moved to Barcelona, Spain, with his family after FC Barcelona offered to pay for his medical treatments for growth hormone deficiency and included him in their youth academy, La Masia.

10 His initial contract with FC Barcelona was famously signed on a paper napkin. This unconventional agreement, by FC Barcelona's technical secretary Carles Rexach, symbolized the club's immediate and decisive commitment to Messi's extraordinary talent.

11 In February 2002, after joining Barcelona's youth academy, La Masia, at age 13, Lionel Messi was officially enrolled in the Royal Spanish Football Federation (RFEF). This formal registration marked a significant step in his journey, legitimizing his status as a player within the Spanish football system and paving the way for his professional career.

12 Messi signed his first official contract with FC Barcelona in June 2004. This contract solidified his status as a professional player with the club.

13 Lionel officially appeared for FC Barcelona's first team on October 16, 2004, in a La Liga match against Espanyol. Entering the game in the 82nd minute, the 17-year-old Messi marked his debut in professional football.

14 Lionel Messi scored his first official goal for FC Barcelona on May 1, 2005, in a La Liga match against

Albacete Balompié. Coming off the bench, Messi found the net with a skillful lob over the goalkeeper, assisted by Ronaldinho.

15 Messi won his first La Liga trophy with FC Barcelona in the 2004/05 season. During that season, he made 7 appearances, all as a substitute, and scored 1 goal.

16 In 2005, Lionel Messi distinguished himself at the FIFA World Youth Championship by winning both the Golden Ball, awarded to the tournament's best player, and the Golden Shoe, for being the top scorer with 6 goals.

17 Lionel Messi's journey with the Argentine national team began in 2005 with his debut in a friendly against Hungary, where he was notably sent off just one minute after entering the field, sparking debates about the red card's fairness. He scored his first international goal in his sixth appearance for Argentina during a friendly match against Croatia on March 1, 2006.

18 Lionel scored his first UEFA Champions League goal against Panathinaikos on November 2, 2005. He became the youngest player to score a hat-trick in the tournament at 19, showcasing his talent in a match against Real Madrid in March 2007.

19 In the 2005-2006 season, at 18, Messi won his first Champions League trophy with FC Barcelona. He contributed 1 goal and 1 assist in 6 appearances. Still, he missed the final against Arsenal due to injury in a

campaign that ended with Barcelona securing the title.

20 On March 10, 2007, in an El Clásico match against Real Madrid, Lionel Messi scored his first career hat-trick, resulting in a 3-3 draw. This performance made Messi the first player since Iván Zamorano (who did so for Real Madrid in the 1994-95 season) to score a hat-trick in an El Clásico match. This feat was particularly notable as Messi was only 19 years old at the time.

21 On April 18, 2007, in a Copa del Rey semi-final match against Getafe, Lionel Messi scored a goal often regarded as one of the best in football history and has been celebrated by many Barcelona fans as the best in the club's history. Messi started with the ball near the halfway line on the right side, sprinted about 197 feet

(60 meters), evaded five defenders, and then scored with an angled finish.

22 In the 2008-2009 season, Lionel Messi was instrumental in FC Barcelona's first-ever treble, winning La Liga, Copa del Rey, and the UEFA Champions League. Messi's standout performances, including being the top scorer in the Champions League, solidified his status as one of the world's premier footballers.

23 On August 23, 2008, Messi played a crucial role in Argentina's Olympic gold medal victory at the Beijing Games. In the final against Nigeria at the Bird's Nest stadium, watched by over 89,000 fans, Messi provided an assist in the 1-0 win. This victory marked Argentina's consecutive Olympic football titles, following their win in 2004, making them the first team to achieve back-to-back Olympic golds in football since Uruguay in 1924 and 1928.

24 Lionel Messi won his first Ballon d'Or in 2009 at age 22, recognizing him as the world's best player following his pivotal role in FC Barcelona's historic treble-winning season.

25 2010 Lionel Messi retained the Ballon d'Or, winning it for the second consecutive year. His consistent high-level performances throughout the year for both FC Barcelona and the Argentine national team were crucial in earning him this honor again.

26 In 2011, Messi achieved a remarkable feat by winning the Ballon d'Or for the third consecutive year. His exceptional performances, including key contributions to FC Barcelona's Champions League victory and La Liga triumph.

27 On March 7, 2012, Messi achieved an unprecedented feat in the UEFA Champions League, scoring five goals in a single match against Bayer Leverkusen. This remarkable performance made him the first player in the competition's history to score five goals in a single game. At that time, no one had achieved such a remarkable milestone in the Champions League.

28 In the 2011-2012 season, Messi continued to break records and collect individual awards. He scored an astounding 73 goals for Barcelona across all competitions, breaking Gerd Muller's longstanding record for the most goals in a calendar year. This remarkable achievement earned him his fourth consecutive Ballon d'Or award, cementing his status as one of the greatest footballers of all time.

29 On March 20, 2012, Messi achieved yet another historic milestone in his career when he became Barcelona's all-time top scorer. At just 24, Messi surpassed the 57-year-old record held by Cesar Rodriguez by scoring a hat-trick against Granada, bringing his total to 234 goals for the club.

30 In the 2014 FIFA World Cup held in Brazil, Messi played a crucial role for Argentina's national team. He

led his country to the World Cup final, scoring four goals in the tournament and providing numerous assists. Although Argentina ultimately finished as runners-up, Messi's performances earned him the Golden Ball award.

31 On November 22, 2014, Messi etched his name even deeper into football history by becoming the all-time top scorer in La Liga. During a match against Sevilla, Messi scored a mesmerizing hat-trick, surpassing the 59-year-old record held by Telmo Zarra with 252 goals in La Liga.

32 In the 2015 Copa América, Messi led the Argentina national team to the final. However, despite his outstanding performances throughout the tournament, Argentina faced a heartbreaking defeat in the final match against Chile. The final ended in a

0-0 draw, and Chile emerged victorious 4-1 on penalties. Messi scored Argentina's only penalty in the shootout, while Gonzalo Higuain and Ever Banega missed their spot-kicks. Despite the disappointment of losing the final, Messi's exceptional contributions earned him the Player of the Tournament award, with 1 goal and 3 assists.

33 On April 23, 2017, Lionel Messi achieved a historic milestone by scoring his 500th goal for Barcelona in all competitions. He accomplished this feat during a thrilling El Clásico match against Real Madrid at the Santiago Bernabéu stadium. In a highly intense and dramatic match, Messi scored twice, with his 500th goal coming in overtime, securing a crucial 3-2 victory for Barcelona.

34 In December 2019, Lionel Messi made history by winning the Ballon d'Or for the sixth time, setting a new record in the competition's history. He outperformed top contenders like Virgil van Dijk and Cristiano Ronaldo to claim the prestigious individual football trophy once again. Messi's remarkable season included scoring 50 goals and providing 18 assists in 59 games.

35 On December 22, 2020, Lionel Messi achieved yet another historic milestone when he became the top goalscorer with a single club. He surpassed the longstanding record held by Brazilian legend Pelé, who had scored 643 goals with Santos in his native Brazil. Messi achieved this feat by scoring his 644th goal in all competitions for Barcelona during a 0-3

victory over Real Valladolid. Pelé's record had stood for 46 years until Messi's remarkable achievement.

36 In July 2021, Lionel Messi achieved a lifelong dream by leading the Argentina national team to victory in the Copa América. Argentina defeated Brazil 1-0 in the final, securing their first Copa América title in 28 years and Messi's first major international trophy. Messi's contributions were instrumental throughout the tournament, and he was named the Player of the Tournament. He also shared the Golden Boot as the top goalscorer with 4 goals, alongside Luis Díaz, and led in assists with 5.

37 In August 2021, Lionel Messi embarked on a new chapter in his illustrious career by completing a highly anticipated transfer to the French club Paris Saint-Germain (PSG). This move came after Messi's 21-year association with Barcelona, which he joined at 13 and won 35 trophies. His transfer to PSG occurred following the expiration of his contract at Barcelona. Messi made a poignant choice by selecting squad number 30 at PSG, which held sentimental value as it was the number he wore on his Barcelona debut in 2003.

38 In his debut season with Paris Saint-Germain (PSG) during the 2021-2022 campaign, Messi continued to showcase his extraordinary talents. He formed a formidable attacking trio with Neymar and Kylian Mbappé, helping PSG secure the Ligue 1 title.

39 On November 29, 2021, Lionel Messi added to his already illustrious collection of individual awards by winning his seventh Ballon d'Or.

40 In the 2022 Finalissima held at Wembley Stadium, Lionel Messi once again demonstrated his brilliance on the international stage. Argentina faced Italy in this high-stakes match, which pitted the European championship winner against the Copa América winner. Messi played a pivotal role in Argentina's 3-0 victory, contributing with two assists and earning the Player of the Match title.

41 In the 2022 FIFA World Cup final, held at Lusail Stadium, Lionel Messi added to his legendary career by making a record 26th World Cup finals appearance. In a thrilling and closely contested final,

Messi scored Argentina's opening goal with a penalty. However, France's Kylian Mbappé quickly responded with two goals, jeopardizing Argentina's lead. Messi showed his resilience by scoring again in extra-time to restore Argentina's lead, only for Mbappé to level the score once more. With the match tied 3-3 after extra time, it came down to a penalty shootout. Messi once again displayed his composure and skill by scoring Argentina's first goal in the shootout. Argentina eventually won 4-2 in the penalty shootout, ending the nation's 36-year wait for the FIFA World Cup trophy. Messi's exceptional performances throughout the tournament, where he scored 7 goals and provided 3 assists, earned him the Golden Ball as the tournament's best player.

42 In the latter part of his illustrious career, Lionel Messi made a significant move by signing with Major League Soccer (MLS) club Inter Miami. After leaving Paris Saint-Germain (PSG) as a free agent, Messi embarked on a new chapter in his football journey. He signed a two-and-a-half-season contract with Inter Miami, which included an option to extend for a further year, potentially keeping him with the club until the 2026 season.

43 Antonela Roccuzzo and Lionel Messi, both from Rosario, Argentina, first crossed paths as children and grew up together. They began dating during their teenage years and maintained their relationship for over a decade before getting married in 2017.

44 Lionel Messi and Antonela Roccuzzo's 2017 wedding in Rosario, Argentina, was a star-studded affair. It featured numerous celebrities and footballers, including Messi's Barcelona teammates Gerard Piqué and Luis Suárez and fellow football stars Sergio Agüero and Neymar.

45 Lionel Messi and Antonela Roccuzzo have three sons: Thiago (2012), Mateo (2015), and Ciro (2018). Messi's social media shares heartwarming family moments, offering glimpses into his life as a devoted family man alongside his football stardom. Notably, the boys show an early interest in soccer, sparking anticipation about whether they may inherit their father's talents on the field.

46 Barcelona served as a second home for Lionel Messi and his family during his iconic tenure with FC Barcelona. While Messi's professional journey took him to various cities, they established deep roots in the Catalan capital. Beyond football, his wife and children embraced the culture, education, and warmth of the city.

47 He founded the Leo Messi Foundation, a philanthropic organization dedicated to improving the lives of disadvantaged children. The foundation focuses on healthcare initiatives, aiming to provide better opportunities and a brighter future for children in need. Through his foundation, Messi has funded educational programs and projects, including the construction of schools and the provision of educational resources. These efforts aim to empower

children with quality education and help them break the cycle of poverty.

48 Messi's charitable work extends to healthcare, where he has supported the development of medical facilities and initiatives to improve the well-being of children facing health challenges.

49 Beyond the foundation, Messi has been actively involved in various charitable activities and donations throughout his career. He has contributed to disaster relief efforts, hospitals, and other causes that align with his commitment to making a positive impact on society. Messi's philanthropic efforts have a global reach, demonstrating his commitment to making a difference in communities worldwide, not limited to his home country of Argentina. His dedication to charitable work has earned him numerous humanitarian awards, underscoring his role as a positive influence both on and off the football field.

50 Messi's star power extends beyond the football pitch. He has endorsed many global brands, including sportswear giant Adidas, soft drink company Pepsi, and technology giant Huawei. These endorsements have not only bolstered his income but have also solidified his status as a marketable icon.

51 Beyond endorsements, Messi ventured into the fashion industry by launching his own fashion brand, "The Messi Store."

This brand offers a clothing and apparel line reflecting Messi's style and taste.

52 Lionel Messi and his family own the "Bellavista del Jardín del Norte" restaurant chain in Argentina.

53 Bellavista del Jardín del Norte is renowned for its delightful ambiance and diverse menu, offering a taste of Argentine culinary traditions. These establishments have attracted both local patrons and international visitors, contributing to Messi's diversification beyond football while highlighting his dedication to Argentine cuisine.

54 Messi's partnership with the Majestic Hotel Group led to the creation of the opulent "Majestic Messi" hotel in Barcelona.

55 "Majestic Mess" hotel, strategically located in Barcelona's heart, attracts tourists seeking cultural experiences and iconic landmarks. With an emphasis on exclusivity, elegance, and premium service, it caters to discerning guests. This venture contributes significantly to Barcelona's tourism industry and local economy.

56 Lionel Messi's art collection boasts diverse works, including renowned Catalan surrealist Joan Miró pieces. These artworks are known for their abstract and playful nature, offering a glimpse into Messi's appreciation for imaginative and emotionally evocative creations that transcend the boundaries of reality.

57 Messi's collaboration with architect Luis Galliussi resulted in "The Messi Collection," a unique furniture line. This venture highlights Messi's passion for interior design, offering meticulously designed pieces that blend aesthetics, functionality, and comfort. "The Messi Collection" allows fans and homeowners to incorporate Messi's distinctive style into their living spaces.

58 Throughout his illustrious career, Lionel Messi has netted an impressive total of 57 hat-tricks.

59 He holds the record for the fastest hat-trick in La Liga history, scoring three goals in just 12 minutes during a match against Rayo Vallecano.

60 Messi has converted an impressive total of 65 free-kick goals.

61 He has scored goals in every minute of a football match, from the first to the last.

62 In football, height varies, but talent knows no bounds. Lionel Messi, at 5 feet 7 inches (1.70 meters), and Diego Maradona, at 5 feet 5 inches (1.65 meters), are revered for their excellence. Meanwhile, Marcin Garuch, standing at just 5 feet (1.53 cm), holds the title of the shortest professional soccer player ever.

63 He has netted 23 goals using his head, showcasing his versatility as a goal scorer.

64 Messi's ambidexterity is a testament to his exceptional footballing talent. While he is famously left-footed, Messi has still netted a substantial 75 goals with his right foot, showcasing his ability to adapt and excel in various situations on the field.

65 He has been clinical from the penalty spot, converting 77 penalties for Barcelona.

66 Messi has found the back of the net from various positions on the field, with 215 goals coming from the left field, 215 from the right field, and 104 from the center field.

67 A significant portion of his goals, 385 to be precise, were scored from within the 6-yard box, showcasing his ability to capitalize on close-range opportunities.

68 While he is known for his close-range goals, Messi has also scored from beyond the 18-yard box, with 24 goals from that range.

69 Messi has not only been a prolific scorer but also a generous provider, recording 205 assists during his time at Barcelona.

70 Messi's remarkable football journey has seen him finish in the top three of the Ballon d'Or voting an astonishing 13 times, securing the runner-up position in 2008, 2013, and 2014. His unparalleled dominance is further exemplified by his record-breaking eight Ballon d'Or wins (Cristiano Ronaldo has five),

solidifying his legacy as the most decorated recipient of the prestigious award.

71 Messi stands alone in football history as the only player to achieve the remarkable feat of winning the Ballon d'Or, FIFA World Player of the Year, and UEFA Best Player in Europe Award all in the same year, accomplishing this extraordinary triple crown in both 2011 and 2015.

72 Messi has consistently earned his place among the football elite by being named to the UEFA Team of the Year an astonishing 12 times, spanning from 2008 to 2020.

73 Messi's supremacy in La Liga has been repeatedly acknowledged, with nine prestigious La Liga Player of the Year awards, recognizing his outstanding

performances in the years 2009, 2010, 2011, 2012, 2013, 2015, 2016, 2017, and 2019.

74 Messi's global impact on the sport is exemplified by his five FIFA World Player of the Year titles, earned in 2009, 2010, 2011, 2012, and 2015, making him one of the most celebrated footballers in history.

75 Messi's exceptional footballing talent has earned him the title of Argentine Footballer of the Year a remarkable 13 times, showcasing his enduring impact on the sport in his home country.

76 Messi had his left foot immortalized in a solid 25-carat gold cast, weighing 55 pounds (25 kilograms) and measuring 10 inches (25.4 centimeters) in height. This golden foot was valued at $5.3 million (£3.4 million) and became a symbol of his footballing prowess. Additionally, a smaller golden footprint was made available for sale at $95,000, and a half-sized gold foot was priced at $42,000. The proceeds from these sales went to the Leo Messi Foundation, supporting those affected by the 2011 tsunami in Japan.

77 Despite his numerous individual football awards and accolades, Lionel Messi has never won the Golden Foot award.

78 Messi has received three red cards in his illustrious career, with two occurring while representing Argentina and one during his time with FC Barcelona. Despite enduring frequent challenges and fouls on the pitch, Messi's three red cards have made

headlines. They are rare occurrences in his otherwise remarkable career.

79 During his youth at Barcelona's La Masia academy, Messi attracted the attention of Arsenal's former manager, Arsene Wenger. Impressed by Messi's potential, Wenger attempted to sign the young talent. However, Messi's status as a budding star within Barcelona's youth ranks was evident, and the Catalan club was determined to retain him. As a result, Messi declined Arsenal's offer and continued his journey with Barcelona.

80 Messi shares a surprising family connection with his former Barcelona teammate Bojan Krkic. They are fourth cousins, with their family ties tracing back generations. Their common ancestors, Mariano Perez Miralles and Teresa Llobera Minguet, married in Catalonia in 1846. Two family branches emerged from this union: one led by Ramon Perez and the other by Goncal Perez. Ramon's lineage eventually led to Lionel Messi, while Goncal's line produced Bojan Krkic.

81 Messi has been awarded the FIFA World Cup Golden Ball twice in his career. He received this prestigious accolade in the 2014 FIFA World Cup and the 2018 FIFA World Cup.

82 In an interview with Paris Saint-Germain's official website, he expressed his preference for playing as a second striker, stating, "I've been used to playing in the centre, behind the leading striker. It's in this position of the second striker where I feel the most comfortable." He further emphasized his love for being actively involved in the game, adding, "I like to always be in contact with the ball. I like to feel that I am part of the game."

83 Despite being one of the greatest footballers, Lionel is reportedly less skilled at playing FIFA on the PlayStation, as revealed by his former Argentina teammate Pablo Zabaleta. Zabaleta shared that during their time together, he often outplayed Messi, who frequently chose Chelsea as his team in the game. Additionally, Zabaleta humorously noted Messi's lack of culinary skills and modest dancing abilities, painting a picture of a football legend with relatable off-pitch traits.

84 Messi's iconic goal celebration, where he points toward the sky with both hands after scoring, is a heartfelt tribute to his grandmother, Celia. She was pivotal in sparking Messi's interest in football and supporting his early steps in the sport. Despite her passing in 1998, Messi's touching gesture ensures that her memory and influence remain a significant part of his football journey.

85 As a young football enthusiast, Lionel Messi idolized fellow Argentine and former Valencia and Real Zaragoza playmaker Pablo Aimar. Their paths

crossed in La Liga matches, with one memorable encounter in 2004 when Aimar, after a game, offered his shirt to the 17-year-old Messi, who was an unused substitute. Messi cherishes that jersey as a symbol of his admiration. In an interesting turn of events, Aimar later became part of Argentina's 2022 World Cup-winning team, serving as an assistant to head coach Lionel Scaloni.

86 Messi's tattoos are personal works of art that hold deep significance. His left shoulder bears a tattoo of his mother's face, a tribute to her unwavering support. He has inked his firstborn son's name, Thiago, on his calf, symbolizing their strong father-son bond.

87 Messi has a few well-known superstitions. One of his superstitions is that he enters the field with his right foot first. He also wears the same shin guards his grandmother bought him as a child. Additionally, Messi typically kisses his tattoo of his mother's lips before stepping onto the pitch as a way to pay tribute to her.

88 Messi has surpassed 100 million followers on Instagram, making him one of the few individuals worldwide to achieve this milestone. His Instagram account is a mix of personal moments, football highlights, and endorsements.

89 Lionel is a well-known pet lover, often sharing his affection for dogs on social media. He has a Dogue de Bordeaux, a breed known for its loyalty and

affectionate nature. He frequently posts pictures and videos of his furry companion.

90 Beyond his footballing prowess, Messi showcases his musical talent by playing the guitar during his leisure time. This hobby is a form of relaxation and allows him to unwind from the demands of his high-profile career.

91 From FIFA 06 to FIFA 10, Messi's rating grew from 78 to 90, reflecting his rise from a promising young talent to one of the top players in the game, eventually peaking at  95 by the end of FIFA 10. From FIFA 11 to FIFA 23, Messi consistently held ratings around 90 to 94, showcasing his sustained excellence. He reached multiple 99-rated special cards in FIFA 19 and 20. Despite a gradual decrease in pace, he remained among the top-rated players, with a rating of 91 in FIFA 23, matching other leading players after his move to PSG.

92 Lionel Messi holds the record for the most appearances on a video game cover by a soccer player, featuring a total of 12 times across the FIFA and eFootball (formerly Pro Evolution Soccer) franchises.

93 Lionel Messi follows a diet focused on hydration and whole foods, including fruits, vegetables, nuts, seeds, and whole grains while avoiding sugar and fried foods. His preferred meal is roasted chicken

with root vegetables, providing protein, complex carbs, and vitamins. During training, he limits meat intake, opting for up to three daily protein shakes and plenty of water to aid digestion, stating that excessive meat consumption is challenging for digestion.

94 Lionel Messi, a native Spanish speaker from Rosario, Argentina, primarily communicates in Spanish. During his over 20-year tenure with FC Barcelona in Spain, he became familiar with the Catalan language, which is prevalent in the region. However, he still needs to acquire proficiency in additional languages, such as English. He has often chosen to express himself in Spanish during public appearances and interviews.

95 Messi follows a structured workout plan to optimize his agility and speed on the field. His regimen includes exercises like lunges, hamstring stretches, and pillar skips for linear speed. For multidirectional speed, he utilizes exercises such as skipping ropes and squats. Messi also works on agility with diagonal hurdles and cone drills, ensuring proper hydration and a cooldown jog to conclude each session.

96 In a high-profile case, Lionel Messi's 21-month prison sentence for tax fraud was converted into a fine by Spanish courts. He was required to pay €252,000, equivalent to €400 for each day of the original sentence. Messi and his father Jorge were found guilty of defrauding Spain of €4.1m between 2007 and 2009, using tax havens to conceal earnings

from image rights. Jorge Messi's 15-month sentence was also replaced with a €180,000 fine.

97 Messi is renowned for wearing the number 10 jersey, a symbol of playmaking excellence, which he donned at FC Barcelona and continues to wear for Argentina. He inherited this iconic number from Ronaldinho in 2008, embodying his role as a leader and one of the greatest players ever. At Paris Saint-Germain, Messi initially wore number 30, his first professional number at Barcelona, before returning to number 10.

98 Lionel is renowned for his introverted personality, a trait that sets him apart in the typically extroverted world of professional sports. Known for being shy and reserved, especially during his early career, Messi's low-key demeanor is reflected in his modest goal celebrations and his preference for a private life away from the media spotlight. This contrast to the typical image of professional athletes has endeared him to fans who admire his focus on football and personal integrity.

99 Lionel Messi holds an impressive 41 Guinness World Records, with some notable ones being: winning the most Man of the Match awards at the FIFA World Cup with 11, being the first person to assist in five different FIFA World Cups, making the most FIFA World Cup appearances as a captain with 19, and having the most appearances in FIFA World Cup tournaments by a male player, participating in 5 different editions.

100 Messi's signature move, earning him the nickname "La Pulga" (The Flea), is a testament to his exceptional agility and quickness on the football field. This move involves his ability to change direction rapidly while keeping the ball closely under control, a skill that has become a hallmark of his playing style. His low center of gravity, combined with extraordinary balance and dribbling skills, allows him to navigate through tight spaces and past multiple defenders with ease.

101 Messi has showcased remarkable versatility and evolution in his playing style. Initially famed for his role as a nimble and skillful winger at FC Barcelona, Messi combined his extraordinary dribbling with precise finishing. Gradually, he transitioned into a more central attacking role, often operating as a 'false nine,' where he blended his playmaking abilities with prolific goal-scoring. Later in his career, including his time at Paris Saint-Germain, Messi continued to adapt, taking on more of a creative midfield role while still maintaining his threat in front of goal. Messi has expressed his desire to play football at the highest level into his late 30s, emphasizing his dedication to preserving top physical fitness and performance standards throughout his career.

6

TRIVIA QUESTIONS

1) What is Lionel Messi's full name, including his mother's maiden name?

a) Lionel Andrés Messi

b) Lionel Cuccitini Messi

c) Lionel Andrés Messi Cuccitini

d) Lionel Messi Andrés

2) At what age did Lionel Messi start playing soccer?

a) 4

b) 6

c) 8

d) 10

3) Where did Lionel Messi move with his family at the age of 13 to join FC Barcelona's youth academy?

a) Buenos Aires, Argentina

b) Madrid, Spain

c) Rosario, Argentina

d) Barcelona, Spain

4) In which year did Lionel Messi score his first official goal for FC Barcelona?

a) 2003

b) 2004

c) 2005

d) 2006

5) Who did Lionel Messi score his first career hat-trick against in a match that ended in a 3-3 draw?

a) Arsenal

b) Real Madrid

c) Manchester United

d) Chelsea

6) What historic achievement did Argentina's Olympic football team accomplish with Messi's help in 2008?

a) Winning their first gold medal

b) Winning back-to-back Olympic gold medals

c) Winning the FIFA World Cup

d) Winning the Copa America

7) In which year did Lionel Messi win his first Ballon d'Or award?

a) 2007

b) 2008

c) 2009

d) 2010

8) How many Ballon d'Or awards did Lionel Messi win consecutively from 2009?

a) 1

b) 2

c) 3

d) 4

9) At what age did Lionel Messi officially sign his first contract with FC Barcelona?

a) 13

b) 15

c) 17

d) 18

10) Which club did Lionel Messi join after leaving FC Barcelona in 2021?

a) Paris Saint-Germain (PSG)

b) Manchester City

c) Bayern Munich

d) Chelsea

11) How many goals did Messi score in a single UEFA Champions League match against Bayer Leverkusen in 2012?

a) 3

b) 4

c) 5

d) 6

12) What record did Messi break during the 2011-2012 season with Barcelona?

a) Most assists in a season

b) Most goals in a calendar year

c) Most hat-tricks in a season

d) Most free-kick goals in a season

13) At what age did Messi become Barcelona's all-time top scorer in 2012?

a) 22

b) 23

c) 24

d) 25

14) Which award did Messi win in the 2014 FIFA World Cup despite Argentina finishing as runners-up?

a) Golden Boot

b) Golden Glove

c) Golden Ball

d) Best Young Player Award

15) In which year did Messi surpass Telmo Zarra to become the all-time top scorer in La Liga?

a) 2013

b) 2014

c) 2015

d) 2016

16) Messi led Argentina to the Copa América final in 2015. What was the outcome of the final match against Chile?

a) Argentina won in regular time

b) Argentina won on penalties

c) Chile won in regular time

d) Chile won on penalties

17) When did Messi score his 500th goal for Barcelona?

a) 2016

b) 2017

c) 2018

d) 2019

18) What significant achievement did Messi attain in the 2022 FIFA World Cup final?

a) Scored a hat-trick

b) Made his 26th World Cup finals appearance

c) Won the Golden Glove

d) Broke the record for most assists in a World Cup

19) In which year did Lionel Messi marry Antonela Roccuzzo?

a) 2015

b) 2016

c) 2017

d) 2018

20) For which brands has Messi been an endorser?

a) Nike and Coca-Cola

b) Puma and Red Bull

c) Adidas and Pepsi

d) Under Armour and Gatorade

21) What is the name of Lionel Messi's fashion brand?

a) Messi Style

b) The Messi Store

c) Leo's Line

d) Messi Wear

22) What is the name of the restaurant chain owned by Lionel Messi and his family in Argentina?

a) Messi's Cuisine

b) Bellavista del Jardín del Norte

c) Argentine Delights

d) Leo's Eatery

23) What type of cuisine is offered at Bellavista del Jardín del Norte?

a) Spanish

b) Italian

c) Argentine

d) French

24) What is the name of the hotel created by Messi's partnership with the Majestic Hotel Group?

a) Messi's Majestic

b) Majestic Messi

c) Barcelona by Messi

d) Leo's Luxury

25) What type of art does Messi's collection prominently feature?

a) Modernist

b) Surrealist

c) Impressionist

d) Classical

26) What is "The Messi Collection" known for?

a) Sports Equipment

b) Clothing Line

c) Furniture Line

d) Watch Collection

27) How many hat-tricks has Lionel Messi scored in his career?

a) 47

b) 57

c) 67

d) 77

28) What is Messi's record for the fastest hat-trick in La Liga?

a) 10 minutes

b) 12 minutes

c) 15 minutes

d) 18 minutes

29) How many free-kick goals has Messi scored?

a) 55

b) 60

c) 65

d) 70

30) How many head goals has Messi scored?

a) 18

b) 20

c) 23

d) 25

31) How much was Messi's 25-carat gold foot cast valued at?

a) $3.4 million

b) $4.2 million

c) $5.3 million

d) $6.1 million

32) Has Lionel Messi ever won the Golden Foot award?

a) Yes, once

b) Yes, twice

c) No, never

d) No, but he was a finalist

33) How many red cards has Messi received in his career?

a) One

b) Two

c) Three

d) Four

34) Which club did Arsene Wenger try to sign Messi for?

a) Manchester United

b) Arsenal

c) Chelsea

d) Real Madrid

35) How is Messi related to his former teammate Bojan Krkic?

a) Second cousins

b) Third cousins

c) Fourth cousins

d) Not related

36) How many times has Messi won the FIFA World Cup Golden Ball?

a) Once

b) Twice

c) Three times

d) Never

37) What position does Messi prefer to play?

a) Winger

b) Striker

c) Central midfielder

d) Second striker

38) Which team does Messi frequently choose to play in FIFA on PlayStation?

a) Barcelona

b) Manchester City

c) Real Madrid

d) Chelsea

39) Messi's goal celebration, pointing to the sky, is a tribute to whom?

a) His father

b) His grandmother

c) His mother

d) His son

40) Which former Argentine player did Messi idolize?

a) Diego Maradona

b) Gabriel Batistuta

c) Pablo Aimar

d) Juan Román Riquelme

TRIVIA ANSWERS

1. c) Lionel Andrés Messi Cuccitini

2. a) 4

3. d) Barcelona, Spain

4. c) 2005

5. b) Real Madrid

6. b) Winning back-to-back Olympic gold medals

7. c) 2009

8. d) 4

9. a) 13

10. a) Paris Saint-Germain (PSG)

11. c) 5

12. b) Most goals in a calendar year

13. c) 24

14. c) Golden Ball

15. b) 2014

16. d) Chile won on penalties

17. b) 2017

18. b) Made his 26th World Cup finals appearance

19. c) 2017

20. c) Adidas and Pepsi

21. b) The Messi Store

22. b) Bellavista del Jardín del Norte

23. c) Argentine

24. b) Majestic Messi

25. b) Surrealist

26. c) Furniture Line

27. b) 57

28. b) 12 minutes

29. c) 65

30. c) 23

31. c) $5.3 million

32. c) No, never

33. c) Three

34. b) Arsenal

35. c) Fourth cousins

36. b) Twice

37. d) Second striker

38. d) Chelsea

39. b) His grandmother

40. c) Pablo Aimar

8

MESSI'S QUIZ SCORECARD

Score ___/40

16-20: Room for Improvement

You're on the right track, but there's more to discover about Messi. Keep learning, and you'll get better!

21-25: Not Bad!

You've got a fair understanding of Lionel Messi. Keep exploring, and you'll improve even more!

26-30: Good Going!

You know quite a bit about Messi. Keep learning, and you'll become an expert in no time!

31-35: Great Job!

You've got a fantastic knowledge of Lionel Messi. Keep up the good work!

36-40: You're a Pro!

Wow, you really know Lionel Messi inside out. You're a true Messi expert!

9

MESSI VS. RONALDO

The Grand Duel: Messi vs. Ronaldo! Who will claim the crown? Stepping into the ring are two titans of the soccer world: the enchanting Lionel Messi and the formidable Cristiano Ronaldo. These icons haven't just shaped a generation of football; they've ignited passionate discussions from street corners to living room couches across the globe. Parallel in their extraordinary skill and enduring presence, they've been the dual dynamos of the pitch, each captivating fans with their distinct and masterful approach to the game. Get ready for an exhilarating face-off across multiple aspects of footballing prowess. Which of these legends will be hailed as the supreme champion of the soccer world?

10

WHO'S THE BEST?

Scoring Spectacle

In the electrifying arena of goal scoring, Messi and Ronaldo have lit up the football stage like no others. Picture this: at the height of their powers, these footballing giants were netting goals with a frequency that left fans and foes alike in awe, averaging an astonishing more than one goal per game!

Cast your mind back to Ronaldo's mesmerizing nine-year stint at Real Madrid. During this golden era, both legends were finding the back of the net every 85 minutes, elevating goal scoring to a sublime level of artistry.

Looking at their illustrious careers as a whole, Messi just edges ahead with an impressive average of 0.78 goals per game, with Ronaldo close behind at 0.72. When it comes to minute-by-minute impact, Messi scores every 105 minutes, while Ronaldo makes a goal impression every 112 minutes.

However, Ronaldo leads in the total goal tally, boasting 869 career goals to Messi's 821, albeit over 154 more games.

Ronaldo evolved from a classic winger to a goal-scoring titan in about 3-4 years, while Messi's transition from a quick winger to a goal-oriented superstar took just 2-3 years. When considering these initial roles, their goal-scoring ratios become even more closely matched.

Assist Artistry

In the captivating world of crafting goals, one wizard stands out. Lionel Messi, with his extraordinary playmaking skills, holds an enviable record that cements his place as a top-notch assistant.

Messi's brilliance has resulted in a remarkable 361 assists over 1,047 appearances, showcasing his knack for visionary play. Ronaldo, keeping pace in the creative arena, has amassed an impressive 248 assists in 1,201 matches.

However, there's an intriguing twist: While Messi's assist count towers, it's easy to underrate Ronaldo's creative flair. His assist numbers, particularly when pitted against other players, are truly commendable.

Taking a closer look at the Champions League, Ronaldo slightly overtakes Messi, having set up 41 goals to Messi's 40, though it took him 20 more matches. This feat adds an extra sheen to Ronaldo's already sparkling record of assists.

Despite Ronaldo's notable performance in Europe's elite competition, Messi's overall assist tally is simply too grand to be eclipsed. When it comes to the finesse of feeding the ball for goals, Messi is the undisputed leader, orchestrating plays with his magical passes!

Precision Playmakers

In the intricate art of precise passing, the statistics point clearly to one maestro: Lionel Messi. Yet, it's essential not to underestimate Cristiano Ronaldo's often overlooked prowess in this area.

Since the 2009/10 season, both on the domestic front and in the Champions League, Messi has excelled as a pass wizard, racking up an impressive 1,393 key passes in 599 appearances. Ronaldo, showcasing his unique style of playmaking, has accumulated a notable 940 key passes in 561 matches.

Messi's talent sparkles even more in executing throughballs, with a stunning tally of 450 successful ones in the same timeframe, significantly outperforming Ronaldo's respectable count of 81.

Despite Messi's clear superiority in these statistics, solidifying his status as the supreme pass master, Ronaldo's numbers are equally commendable. It's intriguing to consider that Ronaldo's passing impact might have been even more pronounced before 2009, a period marked by his deeper involvement in creative play.

In the domain of distributing the ball, while Messi takes the forefront with his unparalleled skills, Ronaldo's diverse abilities on the pitch are unmistakable, further highlighting his adaptability and excellence as a playmaker.

Dribbling Maestros

In the mesmerizing world of football dribbling, Messi and Ronaldo have both weaved their own kind of magic. Ronaldo burst onto the scene as a nimble winger, renowned for his dynamic sprints and deft moves to outmaneuver defenders. However, as he transformed into a formidable inside-forward/striker, dribbling became less central to his style of play.

Messi's journey took a different path. Starting his career along the flanks, he didn't stay there for long. Unlike Ronaldo, Messi transitioned into a more pivotal central role, seamlessly merging the qualities of a classic Number 10 with those of a False 9. This shift meant Messi regularly dropped back to get involved in the buildup, rather than staying upfront.

It's in this deeper role that Messi's extraordinary dribbling skills truly come to light. His ability to navigate through tight defenses is unparalleled, evidenced by his incredible 3,202 successful dribbles in league and Champions League matches, far outstripping Ronaldo's still respectable tally of 1,687 since 2003/04.

In the intricate ballet of dribbling, Messi clearly stands in the limelight. His exceptional control and smooth maneuvering past defenders mark him as the undisputed sovereign of dribbling. While Ronaldo's early career highlighted his dribbling abilities, it's Messi's sustained excellence in this aspect that sets him apart as the ultimate dribbling virtuoso.

Sky-High Dominance

In the aerial dimension of football, the contest for supremacy in heading is decisively tilted in one direction. Cristiano Ronaldo, with his extraordinary aerial prowess, clearly outshines Lionel Messi in this aspect.

Throughout his career, Ronaldo has risen to towering heights, literally and figuratively, scoring a remarkable 146 headers in 1,201 appearances. Messi, whose genius is more rooted to the ground, has managed 26 headers in 1,047 appearances. The contrast in their aerial abilities is not just noticeable; it's monumental.

Ronaldo's expertise in the air isn't confined to just scoring goals. His dominance is further evident in aerial duels, where he has claimed victory in 779 encounters in league and Champions League play since the 2009/10 season, significantly more than Messi's tally of 116.

This divergence in their aerial capabilities is not entirely surprising, considering their physical attributes and distinct styles of play. Ronaldo, blessed with an athletic physique and an impressive leap, is a natural force in aerial battles. Messi, on the other hand, is celebrated for his extraordinary skills with the ball at his feet, weaving through defenses with ease and precision.

In the arena of heading and aerial challenges, Ronaldo indisputably reigns supreme. His ability to command the skies and turn aerial opportunities into goals sets him apart as the unmatched ruler in this domain.

Shooting Stars

In the sharpshooting saga of football, Messi and Ronaldo offer a compelling contrast in their approach to goal-scoring. Ronaldo, the unyielding marksman, has unleashed a remarkable 3,668 shots in league and Champions League since the 2009/10 season. Trailing but not far behind, Messi has launched 2,941 attempts in the same timeframe.

The intrigue intensifies when examining their conversion rates. Messi emerges as the more precise sharpshooter, finding the net every 5.27 shots, a testament to his exceptional accuracy. Ronaldo, meanwhile, scores every 6.43 shots, showcasing his own brand of efficiency.

Looking at accuracy, Messi again takes the lead, with a notable 47.19% of his shots on target, surpassing Ronaldo's 41.19%.

But the narrative takes another turn with Ronaldo's prolific shot-making ability. His relentless barrage of attempts from all angles and ranges, utilizing both feet and his head, speaks to his constant threat on the field. This high-volume approach, combined with his skill in long-range strikes and versatility, evens out the playing field.

In the art of shooting, it's a captivating tie. Messi captivates with his laser-like precision and efficiency, while Ronaldo's expansive and diverse shooting style is equally spellbinding. Their approaches may diverge, but each is uniquely enthralling in its own right.

Penalty Showdown

In the high-stakes world of penalty kicks, a realm where nerves of steel and precision are key, Ronaldo emerges with a noticeable edge over Messi. However, the gap might not be as wide as popular belief suggests.

Ronaldo, often hailed as the unflappable penalty maestro, has racked up 158 successful penalties from the spot, missing 29 across his career. Messi, sometimes unfairly tagged as less reliable, has scored 108 penalties with 31 misses. This puts Ronaldo at an impressive 84% conversion rate, slightly outshining Messi's respectable 78%.

While Ronaldo's numbers are superior, it's worth noting that he isn't infallible. Other top strikers like Lewandowski and Ibrahimovic have shown even higher rates of consistency from the penalty spot.

High-pressure misses? Both legends have had their moments. Messi's notable misses include the 2016 Copa América final against Chile and the 2012 Champions League semi-final against Chelsea. Ronaldo, too, has faced his share of crucial misses, like in the 2008 Champions League final against Chelsea and the 2012 semi-final against Bayern Munich.

In the penalty box face-off, Ronaldo holds the statistical upper hand, but the narrative of Messi being a weak link from the spot doesn't quite hold up under scrutiny. Both have shown remarkable prowess, with Ronaldo just a step ahead in this specific skill set.

Hat Trick Majesty

In the realm of hat tricks, Messi and Ronaldo stand as unparalleled giants, having collectively notched an astonishing 120 three-goal feats. Ronaldo slightly leads with 63 career hat tricks, just ahead of Messi's tally of 57. However, a closer look at their frequency reveals a fascinating twist.

Messi, a virtuoso of multiple-goal games, registers a hat trick every 18.4 matches, marginally outperforming Ronaldo, who hits the hat trick milestone every 19.1 games. This slim difference underscores their exceptional and relentless goal-scoring prowess.

Examining their league game achievements, Ronaldo has the upper hand with 42 hat tricks, surpassing Messi's count of 36. Yet, on the Champions League platform, they are evenly matched, each boasting 8 hat tricks, a testament to their ability to excel on football's grandest stage.

In the exhilarating contest of hat trick achievements, the spectacle is in their scoring dominance. Ronaldo might have the edge in sheer numbers, but Messi's marginally superior frequency of hat tricks brings an added dimension of wonder to this captivating rivalry.

Award-Winning Legends

In the elite sphere of football accolades, Messi and Ronaldo have not only set but continually raised the bar of excellence. Their stranglehold on the Ballon d'Or is simply historic, with Messi leading the charge with 8 wins, eclipsing Ronaldo's noteworthy collection of 5. This dominance is unprecedented in the history of the award, with no other player surpassing more than 3 wins. One can only speculate the heights either Messi or Ronaldo might have reached in their Ballon d'Or tally had they not been contemporaries.

Shifting focus to UEFA's most coveted awards, Ronaldo demonstrates his versatile excellence with 4 major honors, including a UEFA Club Footballer of the Year, two UEFA Best Player in Europe titles, and a UEFA Men's Player of the Year award. Messi, closely trailing, has been adorned with 3 of these esteemed accolades.

In the arena of top scoring, Messi's prowess is highlighted by his 6 European Golden Shoe awards, achieved out of 8 instances of finishing as the league's top scorer. Ronaldo, exhibiting his goal-scoring finesse across different leagues, has topped the scoring charts 5 times, bagging 4 European Golden Shoes in the process.

Ronaldo further distinguishes himself with the Puskas award for the best goal of the year, an honor that has eluded Messi despite his 7 nominations.

However, Messi's luminary status shines brightly on the world stage, having won the World Cup Golden Ball twice, underscoring his pivotal role in Argentina's campaigns in 2014 and 2022. He has also been twice named Copa América's Best Player and once as the Best Young Player.

In this dazzling constellation of individual accolades, Messi and Ronaldo each shine brightly in their own right. Messi reigns supreme in the Ballon d'Or sphere, while Ronaldo displays a broad spectrum of prestigious honors, each illustrating their unique greatness in the football universe.

Trophy Trailblazers

In the dazzling arena of football silverware, Messi and Ronaldo have immortalized themselves, but it's Messi who leads the trophy tally. His remarkable count stands at 44, a collection that sparkles with the 2008 Olympic gold and the 2005 U-20 World Cup triumph, overshadowing Ronaldo's substantial haul of 35 trophies.

Internationally, Messi has soared to the zenith with Argentina, securing both the prestigious Copa América and the iconic World Cup. Ronaldo, Portugal's stalwart, has experienced triumph in Europe, capturing the Euros and the Nations League, adding these accolades to his impressive portfolio.

In the domestic sphere, Messi outshines with 12 league titles, surpassing Ronaldo's count of 7. Yet, in the elite Champions League battles, Ronaldo claims a slender lead with 5 titles, just nudging ahead of Messi's 4.

While the gap in their trophy achievements is slim, Messi edges ahead in terms of the sheer volume of accolades. Each has gathered a remarkable collection of silverware, but Messi's expansive array of triumphs grants him a marginal advantage in this chapter of their legendary competition.

Record Titans

In the extraordinary world of football records, Messi and Ronaldo stand unparalleled, each amassing an array of records that reflect their exceptional careers. Side by side, they match in the total count of records, yet their individual achievements reveal intriguing contrasts.

Messi's record-setting brilliance is epitomized by his surreal accomplishment of netting 91 goals in a single calendar year (2012), a staggering feat that earned him a place in the Guinness World Records. This monumental achievement overshadows his own next highest goal tally of 60, and even Ronaldo's personal best of 69 goals in a year.

Ronaldo, in contrast, commands the Champions League record books. He's at the forefront with the most goals, assists, free kick goals, and shares the record for the most hat-tricks with Messi. Additionally, he holds the record for the most goals scored in a single Champions League season.

At the domestic level in Europe, Messi asserts his supremacy, owning records for the most goals in a single league season (50 goals) and for scoring in the most consecutive league games (21 matches, netting 33 goals).

Internationally, Ronaldo outshines as the all-time leading scorer with an incredible 128 goals, while Messi claims the honor of being the top South American scorer with 106 goals.

In this contest of record-setting achievements, the narrative is one of Messi's remarkable goal-scoring feats and Ronaldo's unparalleled success in the Champions League, each champion setting milestones reflective of their distinctive playing styles and extraordinary abilities.

Global Giants

On the international football scene, Messi and Ronaldo have both forged exceptional careers, slightly shadowed by their club-level exploits but nonetheless strikingly impressive.

Ronaldo, as Portugal's scoring dynamo, impresses with a goal every 127 minutes. Messi, Argentina's pivotal figure, finds the back of the net every 141 minutes. When considering overall impact, Ronaldo contributes a goal or assist every 100 minutes, while Messi slightly surpasses him with a contribution every 94 minutes.

Ronaldo stands as Portugal's all-time leading scorer, having netted an impressive 128 goals in 205 appearances. Messi, closely following, is Argentina's leading scorer with 106 goals in 180 appearances.

Their individual international accolades further underscore their influence. Ronaldo secured the Euro 2021 Golden Boot and the Euro 2016 Silver Boot. Messi, in a league of his own, has earned the World Cup Golden Ball twice (2014 and 2022), becoming the only player to achieve this twice, and has been named Copa América's Best Player twice (2015 and 2021). He also garnered the Golden Boot at Copa América 2021 and the Silver Boot at the 2022 World Cup.

Messi's journey with Argentina includes a mix of heartbreaks and triumphs, with losses in four major finals before securing victories in the Copa América 2021, the 2022 Finalissima against Italy, and the pinnacle of football success - the World Cup. He also holds an Olympic Gold and a FIFA U20 World Cup trophy.

Ronaldo has experienced his highs and lows as well, winning the 2016 European Championships and the UEFA Nations League with Portugal, but suffering a defeat in the Euro 2004 final. He also boasts the record for the most goals in the history of international football.

To sum up, Ronaldo may lead in terms of goal-scoring records, but Messi's vast collection of individual awards, including an unprecedented four Best Player awards at major tournaments, combined with his achievements in the Copa América and World Cup, illustrate the unique and remarkable narratives of two of football's greatest international icons.

Exclusive Offer for Curious Minds!

Immerse yourself in the world of soccer like never before. *Inspiring Soccer Stories* is a collection of heart-pounding, motivational, and awe-inspiring tales from the pitch. From underdog victories to the journeys of legendary players, these stories capture the essence of the world's most beloved sport.

🏆 How to Claim Your Gift

Claiming your free digital copy is as easy as scoring a penalty! Just scan the QR code below, enter your email, and you're all set. We'll send it directly to your inbox!

Made in the USA
Las Vegas, NV
17 December 2024

14719368R00066